20

Restaurants
in
SAN FRANCISCO

20VEGAN.com

Foreword

"It takes nothing from a human to be kind to an animal" – **Joaquin Phoenix**.

San Francisco is undoubtedly a breathtaking city to behold, with its ocean views, colorful architecture, and crazily steep hills. It's also got some delicious vegan food - from entirely plant-based cafes and restaurants, to eateries that have plenty of vegan and vegetarian options.

Officially City and County of San Francisco and colloquially known as SF, San Fran, or "The City," it is the cultural, commercial, and financial center of Northern California. San Francisco is the 13th most populous city in the United States, and the fourth most populous in California, with 883,305 residents as of 2018. It covers an area of about 46.89 square miles (121.4 km2), making it the second-most densely populated large U.S. city, and the fifth most densely populated U.S. county, behind only four of the five New York City boroughs.

San Francisco has always been ahead of the curve when it comes to dining options, and vegan restaurants are no exception. Innovative, plant-centric restaurants have also beenpart of the city for decades and know you can find them in every neighborhood. Bay Area is a culinary paradise with organic farms located just a bridge away. Because of the diverse nature of the cuisine of restaurants in San Francisco, diners can find plenty of restaurants that serve vegetarian dishes in the city. Vegan brunches are becoming increasingly popular with many residents in the town, as well.

In line with the city's vibrant start-up culture, vegan cuisine is taking roots in the City By The Bay. With **40%** of the Bay Area land dedicated to farming, San Francisco has always been spoiled with an abundance of delicious, organic plants.

With the growing number of vegan options in San Francisco, it may as well be on its way to becoming one of the top vegan cities. That's why vegan visitors and residents should be extra excited to dine in the city.

Either you're in the mood for a vegan burger and fries or excellent dining experience; San Francisco will definitely wow you with its vegan-friendly options.

There's a whole lot of options, an entire city filled with so many restaurants that serve equally tasty vegan foods and drinks at pocket-friendly prices too! Considered one of the most "veg-friendly" cities in the US by PETA, San Francisco is not only an oasis of vegetarian and vegan restaurants, according to VegSF, but also has multiple vegetarian and vegan-friendly menus, even at restaurants with meat dishes. You can even eat the fruit that grows on the trees in individual public parks in San Francisco. And with the vegan paradise that is Berkeley right across the bay, herbivores will never run out of dining options.

Lucy McDonald from The Telegraph discovered that the San Franciscans are light years ahead of us when it comes to healthy, vegetarian eating - even if they do drink brassicas for breakfast and their entire food scene is bursting with health.

One of a vegan's heaven is definitely San Francisco; San Francisco is great for all those aspiring to make it big in Silicon Valley, and of course, eat a lot of vegan food. The San FranciscoVeg Society is a non-profit organization that's been championing vegetarianism since 1968. It's no wonder that this city ranks third on the list of cities with most vegans. With more than 20 vegetarian restaurants and countless more that cater to vegetarian and vegan customers, it's easy to find delicious and healthy food made without meat or animal products, whether you live in the Bay Area or are just visiting.

According to research from the University of Oxford, going vegan is the "single biggest way" to reduce your impact on the planet. And that is before you consider the ethical arguments against eating industrially farmed animals, which have an appalling quality of life and are often pumped full of powerful antibiotics that may pose a risk to human health.

The San Francisco Bay Area is among the most vegan-friendly places in the US. Whether you like Chinese, Japanese, or Thai food, San Francisco's got it. Mexican, classic BBQ, healthy smoothies, and delicious vegan cookies—whatever you think of, you'll likely find it here.

Veganism, as opposed to vegetarianism, is a lifestyle: a sort of moral obligation even. Vegans avoid exploiting animals for any purpose, with compassion being a key reason many choose a vegan lifestyle.

Where vegetarianism can – and often does – end at simply omitting animal flesh from the diet, veganism is a moral objection to the use, abuse, and exploitation of animals. For this reason, vegans not only omit animals and their secretions from their diets, but they also avoid wearing animal products: leather, wool or silk, and avoid using any products that have been tested on animals or contain animal byproducts. For example, a vegan would avoid using a lipstick that contains beeswax.

It is the practice of abstaining from the use of animal products, particularly in diet, and an associated philosophy that rejects the commodity status of animals. It is seen as not just a diet but a moral position – perhaps better defined as a philosophy.

According to the **Vegan Society,**

> **"Veganism is a way of living which seeks to exclude, as far as is possible and practicable, all forms of exploitation of,**

and cruelty to, animals for food, clothing or any other purpose."

But, according to the organization, it wasn't until 1949 when Leslie J Cross defined the term, meaning: **"to seek an end to the use of animals by man for food, commodities, work, hunting, vivisection, and by all other uses involving exploitation of animal life by man."**

The Vegan Society was founded in **1944**, but there is evidence of people deciding not to consume animal products over 2000 years ago, but the earliest recorded proponent of this lifestyle/philosophy was **Al-Ma'arri** between **973 – 1057**, but it's important to point out, concepts around veganism and plant-based diets are practically as old as humans, it's just the words that are modern. Archaeologists have even learned some of our prehistoric ancestors didn't eat animals or their byproducts. And across the globe, many groups of people adhere to a plant-based diet for cultural reasons. Although, the most famous proponent recorded was **Donald Watson** – between **1910 – 2005**.

Donald Watson coined the term "Vegan" in **November1944**; when he co-founded the Vegan Society in England. He invented the word by taking the first three letters and the last twoletters of **"VEGetariAN."** The Vegan Society was founded by a group of **vegetarians** who broke away from the **Leicester Vegetarian Society** in England: at this time, the number of people in practice of veganism was below minimum; a lot of them were mostly in the practice of vegetarianism. When **Donald Watson** first used the term, he used it to mean **"non-diary vegetarian,"** and by **May 1945**, vegans explicitly abstained from eggs, honey, milk, butter, and cheese.From **1951**, the society defined it as:

"the doctrine that man should live without exploiting animals."

Interests in veganism increased in the **2010s**, especially in the latter half. *The Economist* declared 2019 **"the year of the vegan."** The Vegan Society says half of all vegans are now aged between **15 – 34,** and more than **60%** of adults have switched to a plant-based diet in the last three years.

The vegan diet has gained momentum in recent years, with more people transitioning to the diet, whether for health or more ethnically based reasons. The vegan diet, often characterized as very restrictive, is associated with health benefits but raises concerns. Controversy regarding the diet exists within the public sphere, with those actively supporting and advocating for it, and those questioning its purpose and anticipated benefits, even disparaging its existence, perhaps because of a lack of knowledge about the diet. This study aimed to provide a fuller picture of the vegan diet, encompassing both the nutrition and health of the vegan diet as well as related ethical beliefs by studying scientific and popular literature in tandem. Furthermore, the study aimed to provide an insider's perspective of the vegan diet as a means of combating stereotypes and making the diet more relatable/understandable to those who are not vegan. By combining all three sources, the project aims to educate the public regarding a diet and lifestyle that is often perceived, at least partially, in a negative manner.

Findings suggest that a well-rounded vegan diet is healthy, and such is evidenced by the variety of whole foods and increased vegetable and fruit intake. Health benefits include a decrease in cholesterol, lipid levels, blood pressure, weight, and a reduced risk for a variety of diseases, including obesity, diabetes, cardiovascular disease, and cancer. Despite the benefits, health concerns do exist, especially in regard to nutrient deficiencies, without a well-planned and varied diet. Nutrient concerns include calcium, vitamin

D, iron, and particularly vitamin B-12 for which supplements should be taken. The nature of the interviews conducted for this paper was such that a comprehensive but diverse collection of information was obtained, precisely because the interviewees have chosen the vegan diet for a multitude of reasons and approach their diet and lifestyle in varied ways. However, there are some commonalities that were revealed. The results of the interview studies demonstrate that about half of the vegans are potentially at risk for vitamin D deficiency because most are taking neither vitamin D supplements nor a multivitamin. Comparing the scientific literature with the interview results reveal that most of the vegans include working out within their daily routines, such that they place emphasis upon physical fitness, suggesting that the vegan lifestyle has benefits beyond merely nutritional. Finally, comparing popular literature to the information gleaned through the interviews conducted establishes that many of the stereotypes regarding the vegan diet are unfounded. The vegan diet is one that is chosen by individuals for various reasons, including health and ethical reasons.

While many health benefits exist, it is essential for those who are vegan or are planning to become vegan to be educated about potential nutrient deficiencies to prevent adverse outcomes. In addition, it is evident that the vegan diet is much more than a diet itself but has developed into a lifestyle, often associated with animal rights and environmental advocacy, as well as a greater concern for physical activity and mindfulness. Further research begs the question of whether the health benefits associated with the diet are solely attributable to the diet or in conjunction with a greater physical activity level and mindful living. With regard to providing an accurate picture of veganism in the popular literature, it is essential to combat negative unsubstantiated stereotypes and myths by providing vegans with unbiased voice with which to share their own stories and beliefs. Lastly, the popularity of the vegan diet and the question of whether it is nutritionally sound, raise issues of anthropologic significance. Specifically, it prompts consideration of whether our ancestral diet was vegetarian in nature, or depended upon meat for evolutionary progress. Moreover, this study demonstrates that the human diet has changed over time, such that our dietary needs, choices, and preferences are inherently reflective of cultural and nutritional anthropology. There are important differences between vegan and vegetarian diets that impact food choice and nutritional intake.The main difference is that vegetarians do not eat meat but will continue to consume dairy products and eggs. Vegans do not consume animal products.This means that it is less necessary for vegetarians to supplement nutrients. They can still get calcium from milk, for example. Vegans, on the other hand, must find a plant-based source of calcium.Veganism also refers to a range of lifestyle choices that exclude animal products, while vegetarianism is purely a dietary choice.

The vegan diet is becoming more popular today – even celebrities and those in the spotlight are making the decision to become vegan. With growing interest in the food, whether among those interested in making the transition to veganism or those just simply wanting to access more information, accurate portrayals of the food are necessary. Easy access to information about the vegan diet can be obtained simply by searching online using one of the many search engines. If this is the year of mainstream veganism, as every trend forecaster and market analyst seems to agree, then there is not one single cause, but a perfect plant-based storm of factors. People cite one or more of three critical motives for going vegan – animal welfare, environmental concerns, and personal health – and it is being accompanied by an endless array of new business startups, cookbooks, YouTube channels, trendy events, and polemical documentaries. The traditional food industry is desperately trying to catch up with the flourishing grassroots demand.

Distinctions may be made between several categories of veganism. Dietary vegans (also known as "strict vegetarians") refrain from consuming meat, eggs, dairy products, and any other animal-derived substances. An ethical vegan (also known as a "moral vegetarian") is someone who not only follows a vegan diet but extends the philosophy into other areas of their lives and opposes the use of animals for any purpose. Another term is "environmental veganism," which refers to the avoidance of animal products on the premise that the industrial farming of animals is environmentally damaging and unsustainable.

Well-planned vegan diets are regarded as appropriate for all stages of life, including infancy and pregnancy, by the American Academy of Nutrition and other bodies in relation to health talks.The German Society for Nutrition does not recommend vegan diets for children or adolescents or during pregnancy and breastfeeding. In concluded research, vegan diets have been seen to lower the risk of type 2 diabetes, obesity, high blood pressure, and heart diseases. An unbalanced vegan diet may also lead to nutritional deficiencies that nullify any beneficial effects and may cause serious health issues.

Some of these deficiencies can only be prevented through the choice of fortified foods or the regularintake of dietary supplements; vegan diets include grains, seeds, legumes (particularly beans), fruits, vegetables, mushrooms, and nuts.

According to a 2016 study, if everyone in the U.S. alone switched to a vegan diet, the country would save $208.2 billion in direct health-care savings, $40.5 billion in indirect health-care savings, $40.5 billion in environmental savings, and $289.1 billion in total savings by 2050. The study also found that if everybody in the world switched to a vegan diet, the global economy would save $684.4 billion in direct health-care savings, $382.6 billion in indirect health-care savings, $569.5 billion in environmental savings, and $1.63 trillion in total savings by 2050.

It should be noted, however, that there is still a difference between vegan and plant-based, even if the two terms are used interchangeably many times in a lot of reports. They both entail eating organic foods, no animals, but for entirely different reasons. Using the term plant-based is more of an umbrella term encapsulating vegans, vegetarians, and flexitarians, where the main focus of their diet is plant foods. There isn't necessarily a moral pressure there; it's merely a diet like raw food or the Atkins diet. So you could be plant-based solely for your health rather than the welfare of animals or environmental reasons. You could be plant-based and still wear leather, whereas a vegan wouldn't, for example. Interestingly, some food that vegans can technically eat like refined foods, people on a strict plant-based diet wouldn't eat –chips, flour, and refined sugar, for example.If you are going vegan, it is essential to make sure you get enough vitamin B12 – commonly found in meat, eggs, and fish – as, without it, you will feel exhausted and weak. You can get B12 from fortified foods, including "dairy alternatives, breakfast cereal, dairy-free spread, and yeast extract," says Heather Russell, a registered dietician at The Vegan Society. Alternatively, you can take a B12 supplement, which you can buy in most pharmacies and health-food stores.People who do not eat meat or fish may lack certain nutrients, especially if they are not consuming eggs or dairy products.

Nutrients that can be lacking include:

Iron

Calcium

Protein

Vitamin D

Vitamin B12

Zinc

Good sources of iron are sea vegetables, such as nori, fortified breakfast cereals, legumes, such as beans and lentils, dried fruit, such as figs, and broccoli, among others. Consuming these with foods high in vitamin C, for example, citrus fruits or tomatoes will help the body absorb the iron.

Supermarkets also improved their selection of vegan processed foods, and even popular chain restaurants across the globe began adding vegan items on their menus.

VEGANISM: WEIGHING THE PROs and CONs

There are literally a thousand and one things you could be, asides being vegan. You're neither of those, just by choice. The life of a vegan doesn't come easy; as there are things that other people find normal but would have to be dropped immediately, we make up our individual minds to take on veganism, but it sure is worth it.

Being vegan isn't only about bringing down the animal industry; it's also about lifting up the vegan movement. Even if you don't try to convince others to go vegan, being vegan makes it easier for others to become and remain vegan in several ways. Briefly: vegans financially support vegan products, spread understanding of veganism, and can be friends to other vegans.

And because vegans are still rare, every vegan makes a significant contribution to all these factors. Going vegan can easily mean being the first, second, or third vegan that your friend knows, and this is a huge deal whether your friend is vegan or not. Being one of a small number of people who regularly buy almond milk at your local store can easily be the deciding factor that convinces them to continue stocking it, or perhaps to offer more similar products.

The more vegans there are, the faster the veganism will grow. And it's already growing fast. There's no doubt that in the future, veganism will be a lot more common, easier, and socially acceptable than it is now. It may even dominate. If you believe that this should happen, don't just sit back and hope it will happen in spite of you. Be the change you want to see in the world.

Every year more and more people are making the decision to go vegan and for a good reason! There are so many amazing ways that veganism can improve our lives – fantastic health benefits, less stress on our environment, more efficient ways to use our resources, and many more!

There are so many unique reasons someone might choose to adopt a vegan lifestyle. When thinking about transitioning to veganism, it's important to ponder your morals and the reasons why this lifestyle speaks to you. A big lifestyle change is easier to sustain if you wholeheartedly believe in your decision. Think about the standards you hold yourself accountable to, and what guides you as you decide what is right and what is wrong.

In the consumer culture we live in today, we show support with money. Every purchase we make is like a vote of support. When we buy commercial products, our money is voting in support of not only the product but also the practices and morals of the company. For this reason, it's important to be an educated consumer so that with every dollar you spend, you're supporting something you truly believe in.

A vegan diet can be one of the healthiest ways to live. Plant-based diets should contain plenty of fresh fruits and vegetables, whole grains, beans, legumes, nuts, and seeds. Because vegan diets often rely heavily on these healthy staples, they tend to be higher in vitamins, minerals, phytochemicals, and fiber. Healthy vegan diets are abundant with vitamins B1, C, and E, folic acid, magnesium, and iron while also being low in cholesterol and saturated fats.

A plant-based vegan diet can reduce the risk of mortality from conditions such as:

- Type 2 diabetes

- Cardiovascular disease

- Ischemic heart disease

- Hypertension

- Stroke

- Obesity

- Some cancers including prostate and colon cancer

Vegan diets can be healthy for anyone of any age, including children, pregnant and lactating women, and the elderly. It's important to note that vegans need to pay special attention to their diets to avoid specific nutrient deficiencies. There is little risk of deficiency in a well-planned vegan diet. For more information regarding vegan nutrition, visit our resource Nutrition on a Vegan Diet. Becoming Vegan by Brenda Davis and Vesanto Melina is also a fantastic resource for ensuring optimal health while living a vegan lifestyle.

There was a time during our evolution when eating meat was necessary for our survival. In fact, it's one of the reasons we're here today! However, our environment won't be able to support our current level of food production for much longer. In 2010, the UN released a report encouraging a global move away from animal products. The report states, "Impacts from agriculture are expected to increase substantially due to population growth increasing consumption of animal products. Unlike fossil fuels, it is difficult to look for alternatives: people have to eat. A substantial reduction of impacts would only be possible with a substantial worldwide diet change, away from animal products."

Breeding, raising, and feeding animals for food is a tremendously inefficient use of our natural resources. Animals raised for food production are fed over half of all the world's crops. As our population grows, we require more and more agricultural space. 60% of worldwide deforestation results from land being converted for use as agricultural land, much of which is used for grazing cattle. An estimated 14% of the world's population (over 850,000,000 people) suffer from undernourishment while we continue to waste valuable agricultural land and resources to produce animal products, therefore obtaining only a fraction of the potential caloric value. Continuing this foolish management of our natural resources is not sustainable.

Following a vegan lifestyle contributes less air pollution and puts less stress on our natural resources by requiring less land, fossil fuels, and water. As the world's population is expected to reach 9 billion by 2050, a widespread movement towards a vegan lifestyle is the most effective way to reduce pressure on our environment and may be absolutely crucial to our survival as a species.

Many people identify themselves as animal lovers, yet intentionally or not; this rarely extends to the animals we use for food. There are a lot of misconceptions about how animal products are obtained, and we often turn a blind eye towards inhumane animal agricultural practices. Animal welfare is an issue we like to push out of our minds, even when it's presented to us in an objective manner.

Factory farming exhibits some of the most severe examples of animal cruelty for food production. Unfortunately, factory farming offers the most competitive prices and makes the most profit, so it's difficult and in some cases, impossible for smaller establishments to survive without adopting the same principles. The competition from large corporations has made it extremely difficult for anyone to offer more humane alternatives, as it is simply not as profitable. Factory farming is an absolutely horrifying business. The focus is on production and profit, the well-being of the animals and workers involved is nearly non-existent. It all comes down to money.

The lives of animals raised for slaughter are miserable, to say the least. The animals are kept in overcrowded areas with little or no room to move, the environment is filthy, and the air is thick with the smell of ammonia and bodily waste. The animals suffer injuries that are often left untreated, from broken bones to burns and lesions from constant contact with their own waste.

With the focus on profit, time is money, which means that the slaughterhouses process as many animals as possible on any given day. It's common for the production lines to be moving so fast that the methods used to kill the animals are rarely effective and cause a great deal of suffering and pain. Because of the quick processing time, many of the animals are still alive, terrified, and in unimaginable amounts of pain during skinning, scalding, and dismemberment.

These are routine practices – millions of animals endure this cruelty and torture every single day, and it's not only the animals that suffer. Slaughterhouse workers are at enormous risk, as well. Cattle often weigh over a ton and are prone to thrashing and kicking, putting the workers in great danger of serious injuries. Many workers have Post Traumatic Stress Disorder and admit to taking out their frustrations on the animals. Workers can also become violent at home, and abuse drugs or alcohol in an attempt to assuage their own guilt and anxiety over what they have witnessed or participated in.

Due to prolonged time spent in these awful conditions, the lives of production animals are as bad, if not worse, than the animals raised for slaughter. Again, the focus is on profit – by minimizing the amount of space and time it takes to obtain animal products, profit is maximized.

To maintain milk production, dairy cows must be repeatedly and forcibly artificially inseminated. After birth, the calves are removed from their mothers within 24-72 hours. The sooner, the better as the relationship between mothers and their calves strengthen over time, and the separation is extremely stressful for both animals. Milk that is produced for the calf is harvested for human consumption, and the calves are fed a powdered milk replacement. Calves born of dairy cows are used for different purposes, depending on their gender. Females begin their lives as dairy cows at 13 months of age. Males are slaughtered for veal within anywhere from just a few hours old up to 4 months of age. The veal industry is a direct by-product of the dairy industry.

While a cow's natural lifespan can exceed 20 years, most dairy cows are killed by the age of 4 and sold as beef. The lifespan of a dairy cow before slaughter is dependent on its ability to produce milk. 90% of dairy cows killed are for reasons such as infertility, mastitis (infection of 1 or more udders), lameness, and low production levels.

Chickens are selectively bred, either for egg production or meat consumption. Chicks bred for egg production are separated by gender. Females become egg-laying hens while male chicks are useless for egg production and can't be used for meat production, so they are killed immediately after hatching. Egg-laying hens are kept in small, overcrowded cages, sometimes with so little room that the animal cannot even turn around. Cage-free chickens are often kept in large warehouses that are so crowded that the animals are debeaked to prevent cannibalism in the flock.

Commercial egg producers sometimes practice forced molting on entire flocks of hens. Forced molting is achieved by removing food and starving hens for 1-2 weeks and also occasionally includes water deprivation. This results in better egg quality, with only a slight reduction in the quantity of the eggs produced.

While chickens can live for more than ten years, egg-laying hens are slaughtered between the age of 2-2.5 years old, as this is when egg production begins to decline.

Again, this is a very brief overview of only some of the inhumane practices of animal agriculture.

The suffering endured by these animals is of unimaginable magnitude. Some people may choose to buy organic "humane" or "cage-free" meat, dairy, and eggs; unfortunately, these terms aren't regulated and are used to mislead consumers. For the most part, buying these "humane" animal products is simply a waste of money as the animals' lives aren't much, if any, better than their "inhumane" counterparts.

There are many ways in which our society exploits and tortures animals, from animal testing to the use of furs and leather. There are many resources at the end of this post so that you can do your own research and come to your own conclusions.

Regardless of concerns over animal cruelty in factory farms, there's another issue at hand when considering animal welfare. Should we be treating animals as commodities at all? As humans, do we reserve the right to use animals as we please? Many vegans believe that we should not. We no longer need to rely on animals for food or clothing, so it does seem self-indulgent to continue to put our cravings, appetites, and desires ahead of the lives and well-being of other living creatures. This issue is one where people tend to either agree or disagree, and it's often very difficult to sway someone to agree with your point of view. It's something that deserves a little research and time spent to decide where you stand on the issue.

There are many arguments made against veganism. However, most of them manage to be both invalid and irrelevant. Widespread veganism is absolutely crucial to our survival as a species. Veganism has little to do with the food chain, what "nature" intended or biological factors. The issue with these arguments is that they don't address the relevant reasons to adopt a vegan lifestyle and instead focus on trivial matters.

When it comes down to it, following a plant-based diet is healthy for our bodies and the environment.

In this day and age, we do not require animal products for sustenance, clothing, or shelter.

We are currently wasting mass amounts of resources by using them to support the growth of animals we intend to kill. These are resources that could be used to feed undernourished people in the world and could be part of the solution to famine.

Things have changed drastically since our hunter-gatherer days. We're now producing such a vast quantity of animal products that we are decimating our natural resources and destroying our environment. Widespread veganism is now fundamentally crucial to our survival as a species.

All animals are sentient beings and are capable of feeling pain and a wide range of emotions, including fear, sadness, and loneliness. If you feel disturbed at the idea of animal abuse against dogs and cats, you must try to understand that cows, pigs, chickens, and other animals used for food production are no different. Food production animals are being abused and tortured, and that is putting it lightly. When you spend money on meat, eggs, dairy, animal-based products, products that employ animal testing, animals at entertainment, etc., you are effectively saying to that company, "I support what you are doing," and what they are doing is abusing animals for profit.

There are a wide variety of resources available for learning about why more and more people are deciding to go vegan. There are some very informative documentaries, books, and websites that are worth looking into.

It's very upsetting and often distressing to look behind the curtain of the animal agriculture industry. If this is your first-time researching animal welfare issues, please prepare yourself to experience a wide range of emotions. It's very common to feel deep sadness and a lot of anger as you learn more. I encourage you to look into these issues because it's important that whether or not you choose to transition to a vegan lifestyle, you are at least aware of the steps that were taken to produce the food or products that you eat or use. Some of the most powerful "light bulb" moments in most non-vegans' lives come from seeing hidden camera footage of the treatment of food production animals, which is horrifying, to say the least.

There's a lot of benefits, as regards taking up the vegan lifestyle, but one shouldn't forget that there are also demerits.

It's not just meat sales declining. The dairy industry has been a vocal opponent of the rise in veganism, as more consumers are turning to plant-based alternatives for health, ethical, and environmental reasons. Sales of cow milk have dropped 11% in parts of Europe, while veganism has been named as a 'threat' to Australia's dairy industry. And with an ever-growing pool of vegan alternatives for well-loved products (for example, Cornetto's vegan ice cream cone and Domino's new vegan cheese), some experts have predicted that the dairy industry could become obsolete in just ten years. Sales of cow milk have dropped 11% in parts of

Europe, while veganism has been named as a 'threat' to Australia's dairy industry.

And with an ever-growing pool of vegan alternatives for well-loved products (for example, Cornetto's vegan ice cream cone and Domino's new vegan cheese), some experts have predicted that the dairy industry could become obsolete in just ten years.

Any diet that involves entirely eliminating multiple food groups can be difficult to follow, and it doesn't work for everyone, so before choosing or deciding to go vegan, make sure to consult with your doctor to see if it is practical based on your current health and lifestyle. A vegan diet might also increase your risk for osteoporosis or low bone density and bone fractures, according to Vanderbilt University Health Psychology Department. Vegans tend to have lower levels of calcium and vitamin D than non-vegans.

However, vegans with high calcium intake have similar fracture risk to non-vegans. If you adopt a vegan diet, pay extra attention to high-calcium foods, such as kale, collard greens, bok choy, and broccoli. Oranges are also a good vegan-friendly source of calcium, and much commercial soymilk, cereals, and pasta are fortified with calcium. Low calcium and vitamin D levels in vegan diets may lead to rickets in children, a condition characterized by soft and deformed bones. The form of iron in plants is less easily absorbed than that from animal foods. Components of plants, such as fiber, phytates, and tannins, further decrease iron availability from plants. As a result, vegans need to take extra effort to plan their diets to include sufficient quantities of high-iron plant foods, such as soybeans, blackstrap molasses, lentils, and spinach. Vegans are also at risk of zinc deficiency. Found in low quantities in plant foods, zinc is subject to the same absorption impediments as iron.

What would happen to the environment if the world population decided to become vegetarian? The answer is not so simple.

- Livestock products provide one-third of humanity's protein intake.

- Livestock production — including food, fiber, fertilizers, energy, and labor — accounts for 40 percent of agricultural GDP and creates a livelihood for 1 billion of the world's poor while employing 1.3 billion people.

- An estimated 20 percent of the total land for livestock production is being degraded by grazing activities; 70 percent of land degradation occurs in arid regions.

- Nearly 30 percent of Earth's ice-free surface is devoted to livestock production, while only 8 percent is devoted to crops consumed directly by people.

- Livestock production deeply impacts air quality, being responsible for over 60 percent of global anthropogenic ammonia emissions (from fertilizers), which contribute to acid rains and acidification of ecosystems.

- Livestock production is associated with 18 percent of greenhouse gas emissions, including 9 percent of carbon dioxide, 37 percent of methane and 65 percent of nitrous dioxide.

- There is an increased risk of diseases transported from livestock to humans

In some poor regions, meat and milk consumption is the only reliable source of protein and fat. Also, in poor regions, many people work with livestock. They could be redirected and trained for farming, but due to limitations with soil quality, this may not be an easy shift. It is important to know that less meat is good, morally, and environmentally, but no meat at all may not be as good as some may think.

Plants may not be sentient beings, but they still feel fear and know a threat when they are dealt with it. So vegans are causing harm to plants when they eat them, as much as meat-eater does to animals. Opponents of the plant-based diet argue that eating meat is not unethical or cruel, but a natural part of life's cycle and every organism on earth dies one way or another. Soybeans, which is a staple protein source in a vegetarian diet, is a contributor to topsoil loss in the U.S.

Because farmers grow genetically modified soybeans, they have to douse their fields with huge quantities of herbicides that are toxic to fish and other plants. So, the idea that veganism is good for the environment may not be entirely true.

Refraining from something that causes so much harm and suffering is laudable, but there's one argument occasionally used in vegan and animal rights campaigns that warrant closer attention – the idea that consuming other creatures is morally wrong in its own right. Opposing meat-eating on **ontological grounds** – meaning, simply because animals are sentient beings, we shouldn't eat them – separates humans from nature and prevents truly ethical relationships between humans, animals, and the natural world.

The late environmental philosopher **Val Plumwood** coined "ontological veganism" to describe this absolute opposition.

Ontological veganism asserts that beings that count as ethical subjects should not be eaten in the same way, that there's a widespread taboo about eating humans. While this thinking erects another unhelpful boundary between animals and other life forms, it's also ironic that the underlying rationale taboos against eating humans are the desire to radically separate humans from other animals.

By framing the consumption of other living beings as an inherent moral wrong, ontological veganism also risks demonizing predation. In order to avoid this, a common approach is to "excuse" animal predation by arguing that the latter is part of "nature," while humans, as cultural beings, should be exempt.

Above all, livestock is essential to many of the world's poorest people and can't simply be cast aside. In low- and middle-income economies, where livestock accounts for 40-60% of agricultural GDP, farm animals provide livelihoods for almost 1 billion people, many of whom are women. Cows, goats, sheep, pigs, and poultry are scarce assets for these people, bringing in regular household income and can be sold in emergencies to pay for school or medical fees. For those who would otherwise have to subsist largely on cheap grains and tubers – risking malnutrition and stunted children – livestock can provide energy-dense, micronutrient-rich food. Animal-source foods are especially important for <u>pregnant women, babies in their first 1,000 days of life, and young children</u>.

When so many lives and livelihoods depend on these animals, should we really envision a scenario where an African household is denied the chance to raise a few chickens or a couple of stall-fed dairy cows? Or an Asian family is prevented from keeping a dozen pigs on a tiny plot? Or pastoralists are prevented from herding goats, sheep, and cattle across drylands? These challenges, all of which are being addressed today in multi-institutional initiatives, should not persuade us to turn away from livestock. They should instead encourage us to pay much greater attention to the sector, enabling it – through scientific advances and enlightened policymaking – to provide the greatest benefits for the world's people at the least cost environmentally and socially.

The main idea behind veganism is to do as little harm as possible. Realistically, it's impossible to live a life that's totally neutral and in which you do no harm at all. Instead, veganism is all about keeping the damage as low as possible so that future generations can continue to enjoy the planet, and hopefully, each individual would learn to make the choices they deem right, both for their sake and that of the environment at large.

SHIVEN VEGAN SUSHI BAR AND IZAKAYA

As most commonly mistaken, sushi doesn't just mean having to do with fish.

Shiven Vegan Sushi Bar and Izakaya is by far one of the most popular vegan spots in the whole of the city of San Francisco. Located at 370 14th Street (at Valencia Mission District), California, USA, the vegan sushi bar was opened in January 2015.

If you have never had vegan sushi, or the concept of such seems a little weird, it'll all make sense once you step inside the "minimalistic den of wooden planks and air plants."

As a top-rated vegan restaurant in the city, it is both an upmarket vegan sushi bar and a Japanese izakaya restaurant with a very modern ambiance, that uses classic Buddhist-style as well as a bunch of locally sourced seasonal ingredients.The dishes are definitely delicious and contemporary, as there is a combination of classic shojin and sushi techniques with local, seasonal ingredients to create healthy and flavorful dishes.

All dishes at this upscale spot are vegan, served in artistic arrangements almost beautiful to eat. Shizen is one of the Bah Area's most acclaimed vegan restaurants. The atmosphere is perceived to be casual, romantic, cozy, or even upmarket: depending on you. There's often a wait to be seated; however, their app lets you know where you are on the list, and there's plenty of exciting shopping in the vicinity.

Among all, their delicious and finger-licking dishes, the green mango nigiri with citrus avocado puree is worth a try, as is the "plot twist" tempura roll with sweet potato, smoked bean curd, pickled mango, tomato, onion, yuzu, shiso, and jalapeño.

The Shizen was opened as a thoughtful path toward ocean conservation.

GOLDEN ERA
VEGAN
RESTAURANT

The Golden Era Vegan Restaurant has been doing business in downtown San Francisco since **1999**. It is a long-time established pure veg Asian cuisine restaurant, which moved from its former location on O'Farrell Street in 2014 to **395 Golden Gate Avenue and Larkin Street**. The restaurant lies in close proximity to the San Francisco City Hall and other places of interest in the area, such as the Federal Building, Asian Art Museum, and the Opera House.

The restaurant is well known for its splendid foods and services. It has an expensive menu that includes a great variety of popular and traditional dishes, beverages, and homemade desserts. The meatless substitute dishes are especially beloved, and pair well with teas and fresh juices. Over the years, Golden Era has continuously evolved and is adapting to the fast-growing trend of healthy living and diets. Foods served are wholesome, and of high quality and are natural and 100% plant-based. Most of the dishes served feature the delicious flavors of the Vietnamese, Chinese, Indian, and Thai. This obviously includes absolutely no MSG, eggs, honey, nor dairy products of any kind.

The Golden Era pleases vegan diners who are fond of traditional Asian recipes because it recreates the meat ingredients by using soy and spices. Their dessert menu is also unusually extensive for an Asian restaurant.

The spacious dining room is not only clean and beautiful, but it is also well designed to accommodate a large seating capacity, and the atmosphere serves as casual and cozy.

It is famous for its style of casual dining and affordable prices. These properties attract tourists, mostly, and other groups of residents.

GRACIAS MADRE

Located at 8905 Melrose Avenue, West Hollywood, CA 90069, United States, the Gracias Mandre is a meatless Mexican restaurant, all vegan and organic, plus a big tequila and drink menu, in a chic space.

This place is always absolutely buzzing with people, with a queue stretching all the way to the door. The menu is entirely plant-based, with dishes loaded with hearty beans, nut-based cheeses, veggies, and a whole lot of flavor.

Gracias Madre's menu is seasonal and is determined by what is currently available at their own organic farm in Pleasants Valley, California.

The Gracias Madre is an airy and tipsy Mexican restaurant with plant-based cuisine, and a lovely patio and stuff. The space is beautiful, bright, spacious, and almost gigantic. No matter what time of day it is, their patio is unarguably one of the best spots in the city to kick back and realize how cool it is to sit out and chill.

The restaurant is a cross between Mexican chic and Palm Springs casual, and it shows how tasty plant-based Mexican cooking can be. The cocktail menu also includes a list of dozens of tequilas and mezeals to choose from. Their highlights include great coffee, great tea selection, great desserts, and beautiful outdoor seating. But I will recommend their guacamole combined with their truly addictive housemade chips; it is an exceptional start. People would also recommend their black bean burger and young coconut ceviche.

The Gracias Madre is famous for lunch, solo dining, or even group dinners and dinner dates. For tourists, the entire experience seems made for Instagram and to make your friends back home jealous. If there's any downside, some of the dishes can be filling, so pace yourself. And parking can be a challenge, so ride-sharing is recommended.

INDOCHINE
VEGAN
RESTAURANT

This excellent dining institute is situated on **508 Valencia Street, San Francisco, CA 94110, United States**. Indochine came to be about three years ago when the owner was inspired to create an animal and earth-friendly diet for all, a Pan-Asian food restaurant in the Mission District since 2014.

Indochine Vegan offers delicious dining and takeout to San Francisco, CA: Indochine Vegan is a cornerstone in the San Francisco community and has been recognized for its outstanding Dessert cuisine, excellent service, and friendly staff. The dessert menu is known for its modern interpretation of classic dishes and its insistence on only using high-quality fresh ingredients.

Indochine is a prominent traditional Korean restaurant that makes traditional Korean dishes into vegan meals. Dishes fromChina, Thailand, Vietnam, and Japan are also made and sold. It is a comfortable cafe-like space, with a neighborhood vibe featuring vegan Asian dishes, from pho to curries.

Their customer service, as seen through a lot of reviews, is somewhat poor due to a lot of sit-in customers. The atmosphere is otherwise really casual and cozy, and the restaurant is otherwise popular with college students, groups of residents, and tourists for their options of table service, desserts, deliveries, and takeaways.

Their most popular dishes include the Vietnamese clay pot rice, orange sesame fries, and the chow mein noodles.

LOVING HUT VEGAN RESTAURANT

The Loving Hut is an international vegan restaurant group, where each restaurant is owned and operated independently. It was inspired and founded by **Ching Hai**, whose followers call him **"supreme master."**

The loving hut is one of the largest families of vegan restaurants in the world, with more than 200 outlets in major cities spread across the globe. All of the menu items are made with wholesome, plant-based ingredients. Each loving hut is individually owned, with the autonomy to choose its own menu, thus giving a distinctive difference among all locations.

That of interest is located on **524 Irving Street, San Francisco, CA 94122, United States**, a fully vegan restaurant in San Francisco's Sunset neighborhood.It is one of the many vegan counter-serve chains with Asian-accented menus that vary by location.

San Francisco locations include Sunset and Westfield Mall. The Sunset location is closed on Wednesdays, while the Westfield restaurant works seven days a week.

Services rendered include take-outs and dining, delivery, online orders, buffets, and catering services. The restaurant opens up for business at

10:00 am and closes before 9:00 pm, except on Sundays when it closes at 7:00 pm.

The Loving Hut was created with the vision that all beings can live in peace and harmony with each other and the planet. It stands as an accessible starting point for those making the transition to a plant-based diet.

Dining options include deliveries, desserts, table services, or take-outs while the atmosphere appears as really casual, and it is commonly visited by college students and other groups of residents.s

ANANDA FUARA

The Loving Hut is an international chain of more than 140 restaurants, which has been called the fastest-growing vegan franchise in the world, and many consider it to be operated by a cult.

This is a San Francisco vegetarian restaurant offering a variety of Asian-inspired meals alongside Indian dishes and American foods like veggie burgers and sandwiches. A Sri Chinmoy enterprise. Free meditation classes provided. Sri Chinmoy is the driving force behind this celebrated vegetarian and vegan eatery.

Located at 1298 Market Street, San Francisco, CA 94102, USA, Ananda Faura literally translates to "Fountain of Delight," a name was given by the spiritual teacher Sri Chinmoy. Because of his inspiration, the restaurant strives to offer customers delicious food that satisfies inwardly and outwardly in a peaceful atmosphere.

Mostly visited by tourists and other groups of residents, the atmosphere of the Ananda is casual and cozy. They are famous for their delicious breakfasts, lunch, dinners, and even dinner dates! The highlights of the Ananda; asides their mouth-watering menu includes a great tea selection, and a great dessert menu.

What makes the Ananda stand out from the rest is the fact that they honor their founder ever so diligently. The Ananda Faura closes for the second week of April to attend a celebration in remembrance of Sri Chinmoy's arrival to the West, and the last week of August to participate in a celebration of Sri Chinmoy's birthday anniversary.But on normal days, the restaurant opens up at 11:00 am and closes at 8:00 pm.

While visiting the Ananda Faura for the first time, I would recommend the Portabello Quesadilla: a yellow chipotle tortilla filled with sauteed portobello and melted cheese, a side of salsa and black beans.

VEGAN PICNIC RESTAURANT

"We are an American-style deli and grocer with classic comfort food that happens to be 100% plant-based. Simple, quick, and Guiltlessly Delicious!"

-Style deli and grocer with classic comfort food that happens to be 100% plant-based. Simple, quick, and Guiltlessly Delicious.

A vegan picnic sounds like somewhere you'll be served wheatgrass and encouraged to forage for berries — hard pass. Conveniently, Vegan Picnic involves doughnuts, a shockingly passable/borderline delicious "crispy chicken" sandwich, and a Caprese salad with dairy-free cheese. Space is designed to get you to your picnicking stat, with no tables and a counter-order set up.

A few years ago, owner Jill Ritchie found herself starting over after leaving the tech industry and becoming a single mom. While figuring out what to do with her new life, Jill's children decided to become vegan. She joined them the very next day and was disappointed in the quality of food. After curating the best products for her family and experimenting in the kitchen, Jill realized she wanted to share her knowledge with the world. With a new purpose, she began a Vegan

Picnic.The Vegan Picnic is now a grab-and-go spot in Cow Hollow that's perfect for lunch.

Located on 1977A Union St, San Francisco, CA 94123, United States, the Vegan Picnic is alsoa vegan cafe and market for plant-based American deli classics, gluten-free eats, and gourmet groceries.

Traditional American dishes and deli fare get the vegan treatment at this Cow Hollow cafe that serves plant-based versions of fried chicken, egg salad, meatballs, and other classics (including several gluten-free options), along with vegan pastries and gourmet grab-and-go grocery items. Outfitted in white, slate, and blond wood, with counter seating along the front window, the compact space feels clean and modern.

Breakfast is available all day, and the staff members couldn't be nicer, even when they get to serve you with free food samples. If all vegan meatballs, faux crispy chicken sandwiches, and imitation salami subs tasted this good, every cow, chicken, and pig could run free.The Vegan Picnic opens up at 9:00 am every day, and closes at 6:30 pm. Just make sure to try out their whole range of vegan sandwiches and burgers.

VEGANBURG
RESTAURANT

VeganBurg is a vegan fast-casual chain of restaurants, which currently has one outlet in Singapore and one outlet in San Francisco, United States.The product range of VeganBurg includes vegan burgers, hot dogs, soups, salads, fries with seaweed, and desserts.

VeganBurg was founded in 2010 by Alex Tan with its headquarters in San Francisco, located on 1466 Haight St, San Francisco, CA 94117, United States.

It is ahealth-focused and fast-casual Singapore based chain. It aims at bringing affordable meat-free burgers and vegan interpretations of other New American classics in a stylish, modern counter-service cafe.

The outlet in San Francisco was established in 2015. The menu includes a range of vegan burgers and plant-based New American standards, fries, sides, and beverages. Their burger patties are made from non-gmo soybeans and mushrooms.The foods are a mix of vegan, American, and gluten-free. Make sure to give their Haight 'n' Salsa, Mustang relish, and Hawaiian teriyaki a go. Services rendered include fast food, takeouts, lunch, dinners, and brunches in their well-styled counter-serve cafe. The atmosphere comes off as casual and cozy, with a crowd of college students, tourists, and groups of residents. It is also family-friendly.

THE BUTCHER'S SON

SCAN ME

Opened in February 2016, The Butcher's Son reflects a new trend in the plant-based food movement—with the openings of several other vegan butcher shops and delis across the country—proving that even the most traditionally meat- and dairy-based dishes can be made vegan.

The new space, which is 1,300 square feet bigger, comes with a market area stocked with takeout food, more vegan meats, and take-and-bake cheese items like faux-chicken pot pies and lasagnas. They've also partnered with Curbside Creamery for custom ice cream flavors, debuting last week with an espresso brownie made with The Butcher's Son's brownies and Timeless coffee, and a chocolate chip cookie dough ice cream made with Butcher's Son cookie dough.

It is an all-vegan delicalessen located at **1954 University Avenue, Berkeley, CA 94704**, the United States with canou, coffee, veggie platters, and sandwiches in creative combinations.

Started by brother-and-sister duo Christina Stobing and Peter Fikaris about two-and-a-half years ago, the Butcher's Son has been extremely popular ever since. They had been thinking about a second location when Maker's Common closed across the street in March. Instead of opening a second location, they decided to expand on what they already have going on and made it even better.

The Butcher's Son makes almost all of its vegan meats and cheeses in-house and offers an extensive menu of sandwiches, salads, and other offerings. Between the pulled pork sandwich, chicken parmesan in a garlic bread roll, and tuna melt, the Butcher's Son ensures that vegans do not miss real meat. Everything on the menu is free of animal products — the house-made cheeses are cashew-based, and other common ingredients are almonds, gluten, coconut, and soy (their menu comes with a significant warning sign for allergies).

The shop's cheeses are one of the standouts. The cheeses they make, from buffalo mozzarella to pepper jack, have an incredible texture that even melts like dairy cheese — a far cry from most grocery store-bought vegan cheeses. They also carry Violife's cheddar cheese, which is free of common allergens like gluten, soy, and nuts.

The updated menu includes vegan fish, which wasn't previously offered — smoked whitefish and catfish, to be exact, which both come in sandwich form like their blackened Cajun catfish

Being a comfortable space with exposed brick, big windows, and tall, open-beamed ceilings, it is a charming, industrial-chic bakery and diet for pastries, coffee, and creative vegetable-based mains.

The Level 8 Vegan, a toasted bagel with fried chicken, bacon, cream cheese, lettuce, tomato, and avocado, is a must-eat dish.

CYBELLE'S FRONT ROOM

Cybelle'sis located on **1385 9th Avenue, San Francisco, CA 94122, United States**.

They specialize in New York pizza styles alongside a vegan menu that includes cashew cheese, cashew pesto, vegan parmesan, mushroom bolognese, and stuffed mushrooms. Pizza toppings include a plant-based lemon pepper shrimp and come with a side of their housemade vegan garlic parmesan made from roasted cashews. They also have a list of vegan beers all for sale on the menu.

Asides their big hefty slices of NY-styled pizza, they also indulge in other Italian eats in a tavern setting that's also kid-friendly.

Services rendered include lunch, dinners, solo-dining, delivery, desserts, table services, and takeouts on all days except Tuesdays when they are always closed, with a casual and cozy atmosphere. College students and other groups of residents are their primary customers.

NICK'S KITCHEN

Known for their popular homestyle vegan Filipino food in Daly City, the co-owners of Nick's Kitchen have opened their second location. Sitting pretty on **223Grand Avenue in South San Francisco,** regulars will be happy to note that the new location will offer the same classics as the first Nick's. That means everything from vegan Lumpia Shanghai and Sizzling Sisig to Halo-Halo and Leche Flan will now grace the plates of San Mateo's health-conscious crowd. The only vegan restaurant in South San Francisco, Nick's On Grand, does many things, but one thing is for sure; it puts plant-based food on the map for a bustling city that's long overdue.

Located just five minutes from San Francisco Airport, and nearby numerous hotels and well-known biotech companies, Nick's On Grand adds a neighborhood feel. Its co-owner, Kenny Annis, designed and built the new location purely on his own steam. As a result, co-owner and chef Reina Montenegro says, "This place is magical. It's built purely with love." Co-Owners Reina Montenegro and Kenny Annis purchased their first restaurant in 2015 and converted it to a vegan menu in 2017. Only ten minutes away from the original Nick's Kitchen, the new restaurant added numerous salads and gluten-free options to their plant-based menu.

What makes the restaurant stand out from the others is its indulgence in live music and its toleration space for the LGBTQ community and other transgender people.

The new location is more prominent and with a lovely back patio. The menu is similar to the former with lunch options and Filipino favorites like pancit and caldereta. Their Jackfruit rib plate is a must-try!

NOURISH CAFÉ

Nourish Cafe has two locations in San Francisco: 189 6th Avenue (near California)

San Francisco, CA 94118 and on 1030 Hyde Street (near California)

San Francisco, CA, 94109, United States. The 100% plant-based menu is based on foods derived from plants, including vegetables, whole grains, nuts, seeds, legumes, and fruits. There is a use of sustainable, local ingredients on the menu that make a low carbon impact. They also use compostable takeout containers, straws, and cutlery, and fill up giant, green compost bins every night.

Nourish Cafe opened in 2015 and is owned by Sarah Bacon and Brighton Miller. Head Chef Brighton Miller is a professionally trained natural chef. Bacon is an entrepreneur, and General Manager at Nourish focused on the business and operations of the cafe. Both are passionate about eating healthy and sharing that with customers.

Nourish Cafe is 100% plant-based and uses organic, whole foods and non-GMO ingredients to create delicious, wholesome, and healthy foods; they use only natural sweeteners and minimal oils. It's located in Inner Richmond, between Presidio and Golden Gate Park, and it's really tiny, especially when it's somewhat cold outside since it can fit only ten people inside. They have huge salad bowls, big sandwiches and wraps, delicious toasts, and big smoothies (you can find the complete menu here). Desserts and sweet treats are out of the menu and shown on the counter. They also have daily specials on a blackboard.

It's one of the places we go when we want to chill out in a quiet place or when I want to look for some cookbooks at the Green Apple Books, or we need a walk in nature, out of the chaos of the city.

Once visiting, never forget to try their famous Golden Gate Bowl; Jasmine brown rice, cabbage, avocado, yams, roasted broccoli and cauliflower, roasted mushrooms, mixed greens. Red pepper almond dressing.

GREENS'
RESTAURANT

Greens Restaurant is a landmark vegetarian restaurantin the Fort Mason Center in the Marina District, San Francisco, California, overlooking the Golden Gate Bridge.

Founded by the San Francisco Zen Center in 1979,Greens has been credited in The New York Times as "the restaurant that brought vegetarian food out from sprout-infested health food stores and established it as a cuisine in America."

Greens were founded by the San Francisco Zen Center in 1979, and the original chef, Deborah Madison, shifted the idea of vegetarian cuisine from bland sustenance to sensational tastes. Chef Annie Somerville took over in 1985 and elevated Greens to the lauded perch it sits on today in San Francisco's competitive restaurant realm. Greens were groundbreaking by using local ingredients from fresh farms and dairies long before it was trendy to do so. The 130-seat restaurant in Fort Mason has views all the way to the Golden Gate Bridge. The menu changes seasonally (so come back often) and presents dishes such as poblano chili stuffed with goat cheese, avocado, and crème fraîche; roasted figs and burrata; or a portion of pappardelle pasta with English and snow peas. After three decades in San Francisco, Greens still blazes a vegetarian trail, and food-savvy San Francisco knows a good thing when it tastes it.

Career carnivores won't realize there's zero meat in the hearty black-bean chili, or in Greens' other flavor-packed vegetarian dishes, made using ingredients from a Zen farm in Marin. And, oh, what views! The Golden Gate rises just outside the window-lined dining room. The on-site cafe serves to-go lunches, but for sit-down meals, including Saturday and Sunday brunch, reservations are recommended.

When in town, don't forget to try out the Gratin Provencal; with eggplant, summer squash, peppers, leeks, basil, point Reyes toma, and Fromage blanc custard. It is served with tomato-roasted garlic sauce, grilled polenta, summer beans with shallots, and pepper flakes.

NEXT LEVEL
BURGER

America's first 100% plant-based burger joint.

The new restaurant joins the recently opened location in Concord, Calif. as the brand's second California-based location; it is seventh overall. The highly anticipated fast-casual phenomenon is located inside the Potrero Hill Whole Foods Market at 450 Rhode Island St. San Francisco, CA 94107.

Founded in 2014 by husband and wife duo Cierra and Matt de Gruyter, Next Level Burger was born in Bend, Oregon. In just four years, NLB has built an out-of-this-world fan base and established a strong following throughout the Pacific Northwest, NYC, and the Bay Area.

Next Level Burger is recognized for its revolutionary menu of plant-based twists on classic burger joint favorites, including over a dozen jaw-dropping burger combinations. Designed to make plant-based eating delicious and accessible for people of all ages, fan-favorite menu items include:

· The Signature Burger, featuring a house-made umami mushroom and quinoa patty topped with avocado, cheddar or swiss-style cheese and roasted garlic thyme mayo

· The All-American, featuring a savory, meaty patty topped with smokey tempeh bacon, cheddar or swiss-style cheese, and egg-free mayo.

Menu items also include next-level hot dogs, sandwiches, salads, and sides, including a variety of fries and tots. A dedicated kids' menu means the whole family can enjoy a better-for-you and better-for-the-planet meal. Dessert offerings include delectable diner-style hand-spun shakes from standard flavors like organic chocolate and vanilla, to next-level flavors like Cookies N' Cream and Salted Caramel Peanut. All shakes are dairy-free, allowing guests the option of a coconut or soy soft-serve base. It's a sinfully satisfying experience without the guilt that any food enthusiast – plant-based or not – will immediately love.

MISSION CURRY HOUSE

An authentic Indian & Himalayan Cuisine.

Located on 2434 Mission Street,San Francisco, California, the highly skilled Chefs offer you traditional Indian cooking, and all of the dishes are made with the freshest available, locally sourced ingredients and the highest quality imported herbs and spices for wonderfully aromatic curry blends.

It is San Francisco's first delivery/take out only Indian fast-casual restaurant, and it sure lives up to the expectations of many of the residents and tourists that frequent the space. Owner Ajay Khadka is behind three other Indian restaurants in San Francisco: Om Indian Cuisine (1668 Haight St.), Tara Indian Cuisine(2217 Market St.), and Royal Indian Cuisine(1740 Filmore St.). For his newest spot, Khadka wants to experiment with a few new ideas, including serving someHimalayan dishes like momo (Nepalese-style steamed chicken or vegetable dumplings).

He also plans to serve organic chicken and vegetables and to offer gluten-free curries and bread. (Check out the full menu here.)

Khadka told Hood line he's long wanted to open a restaurant in the Mission. "I've been in San Francisco for a long time, so now I can finally serve good food in that neighborhood and do the fusion of Himalayan and Indian food that I've wanted to do for years," he said.

Some of their popular and tasty dishes include; the Samosa – homemade crispy Indian pastry stuffed with spiced peas and potatoes, and Jeera Rice – basmati rice, flavored with cumin and turmeric.

WILD SEED RESTAURANT AND BAR

Located on **2000 Union Street, San Francisco, CA 94123, United States.**

It took prolific San Francisco restaurateur Adriano Paganini a few weeks to transform Belga, a Belgian sausage and beer restaurant, into Wildseed, the group's first vegetarian restaurant.

Wildseedopened up on Union Street in Belga's former home, marking the first plant-based business for Paganini's Back of the House, the hospitality group that now runs more than 20 Bay Area restaurants, including the Super-Duper Burger chain, Delarosa, A Mano, and Barvale, among others.

The month-old restaurant in Cow Hollow is the latest concept by the Back of the House restaurant group, whose parade of hits has shown a preternatural ability to anticipate culinary trends: grass-fed fast food burgers (Super Duper), pizza and cocktails (Beretta, Delarosa), gourmet fried chicken sandwiches (the Bird), and now, plant-based cuisine. To see this group putting its chips down on vegan cuisine is very telling of how Bay Area diners will be eating in the next decade. If the future of food is vegan, this spot is a very convincing data point in that theory's favor.

Wildseed is effective because of how well it is camouflaged as your usual trendy neighborhood restaurant. Its folksy decor is anchored in a Pinterest-friendly combination of turquoise and gold; it looks more like an oyster bar than a vegan spot. Its menu, crafted by omnivores, has the potential to appeal to a wide range of eaters.

Case in point: On a recent weekend night, the wait for a walk-in table was two hours. (If you're open to sitting at a communal table in the lounge area, that wait will be heavily truncated; and reservations are available.)

Situated at the nexus of a SoulCycle, an Equinox and five yoga studios, the all-vegan restaurant slots in extremely well with Cow Hollow's wellness worshipers, who flock here for post-workout meals of beet pate, kombucha cocktails, Impossible burgers, and cheeseless cheesecake. According to Wildseed chef Blair Warsham, the management team even joked about putting out a storage receptacle for rolled-up yoga mats.

VEGAN MOB

Toriano Gordon has combined his talents as a rapper, social media entertainer, and chef into Vegan Mob, a plant-based barbecue and soul-food pop-up he started this spring. Vegan Mob's first day as a permanent Oakland restaurant is tomorrow, Saturday, October 5, and you can be sure Gordon is letting all his fans know on his popular Instagram account.

Gordon's boundless energy also helps Vegan Mob's food stand out from the rest of the vegan pack. For him, avoiding meat doesn't mean avoiding fun: "I like to entertain, and I like to cook — I want people to enjoy it."

While Gordon himself is a native San Franciscan, born and raised in the Fillmore, he's excited about his new digs in Oakland. The spot is 500 Lake Park Avenue, the former location of Grand Lake landmark Kwik Way Drive-In, and, most recently, the temporary home of Merritt Bakery. The lot is eventually slated for development, but Vegan Mob's lease will last at least 18 months. And Gordon has made space his own, decorating the front with Vegan Mob's logo in green and white. A mural on the side pays homage to the

Jacka, the East Bay rapper (and friend of Gordon's) who was killed in 2015.

Two years ago, with concerns about his health, Gordon switched to a vegetarian, then a vegan diet. "I treasure my life," Gordon says — and eating well has made him feel healthier than ever.

Vegan Mob's recipes are adaptations of classics like mac-and-cheese and PO' boys, passed down through family members like Gordon's Texas-born grandmother, who opened a cafe in the Fillmore in the '60s, and others like his grandfather on his stepfather's side, who owned Rue Lepic and Nob Hill Cafe in SF. Cooking vegan is simple; Gordon says: substitute out the animal products. In his gumbo, for instance, Gordon swaps in plant-based shrimp and adds seaweed for a fuller flavor, plus imitation bacon for a bit of smokiness.

Some of Vegan Mob's items incorporate Impossible Foods' meat, like Gordon's Impossible Mob tacos, and others use plant-based "brisket" from GW Chew, the Oakland food entrepreneur behind the Veg Hub. Gordon counts Chew and others like Evan Kidera, a childhood friend from SF who founded Señor Sisig, as mentors.

SOULEY VEGAN

Tamearra Dyson, the owner of Souley Vegan, has been cooking her signature plant-based dishes since the age of 18. Located on 301 Broadway, Oakland, United States, Souley Vegan is one of the most popular vegan restaurants in San Francisco as a whole.

One of the best meat-free eateries in the Bay Area prides itself on a cuisine that's typically anti-vegan. Unlike a traditional, fat- and cholesterol-heavy soul food meal, you can completely gorge yourself and count on not feeling too gross afterward. A perfect assortment of comfort style Southern-inspired dishes with a totally awesome vegan menu. The range of Louisiana Creole here is simply incredible and put, non-vegans enjoy the dishes just as much!"

For nearly a decade, Oakland's Souley Vegan has sat on a quiet corner at 301 Broadway (3rd Street) in Jack London Square, serving up healthy, plant-based soul food. The restaurant's menu is comprised "solely" of vegan dishes, meaning that no meat, fish, or dairy products are used.

This vegan soul food diner in Jack London Square is the kind of place where carnivores won't care that they aren't eating meat. Brunch is Souley's standout meal, complete with bottomless mimosas that pair well with blueberry pancakes and sweet potato waffles. The menu covers all the Soul Food classics such as black-eyed peas and southern fried dishes, but Souley Vegan serves southern fried tofu in lieu of southern fried chicken. There's even a touch of the Mediterranean—a couscous plate which includes glazed onions, mushrooms, and yellow corn.

Music does play a big part in creating the atmosphere at Souley Vegan. Soul and jazz from African American artists play over the restaurant loudspeaker as patrons dine. The walls are graced with portraits of black jazz musicians such as Louis "Satchmo" Armstrong. Live music is performed at Souley Vegan on Thursday evenings. Dyson added that she likes to hire people from the neighborhood and that the neighborhood has been supportive of her. Her customer base, she notes, comes from near and far.

Souley Vegan is open Tuesday-Thursday 11 am-10:30 pm, Friday-Saturday 11 am-11:30 pm, Sundays 10 am-3 pm at 301 Broadway in Oakland. Catering is also available.

CHA-YA

Vegan Japanese food inspired by Zen cooking.

Cha-Ya is located on **762 Valencia St, San Francisco, CA, USA**. "Our family opened Chaya's mother restaurant, Hikage Chaya in the early 1600s, as a teahouse along a mountain pass near the harbor city of Kamakura, Japan. The combination of fine fish and spices passing through the port and the preponderance of weary travelers quietly made Chaya into a somewhat famous destination unto itself. When the Imperial Summer Villa was completed in 1893, just minutes away in Hayama, our restaurant had truly arrived. Chaya became a Ryokan and established itself as a gathering place for the royal court, government officials, and for those who sought a summer audience with the emperor.

After endearing ourselves to the imperial kitchen more than one hundred years ago, Chaya quickly evolved into the modern era. In the 1970s, Hikage Chaya was a landmark destination for weddings and formal events. As Japan turned its attention outwards in the 1980s, we opened La Marée de Chaya in a pioneering step towards fusion cuisine.

Consecutively we landed in Los Angeles, opening La Petite Chaya in Silver Lake and Chaya Brasserie in Beverly Hills. Our marriage of French and

Japanese traditions blossomed in the west. One night in 1984 at Chaya Brasserie, the iconic dish Tuna Tartare was born, and throughout the 1990s, the restaurants became beloved haunts of actors and artists.

In 2006 M Café on Melrose Avenue was opened: a casual concept serving contemporary macrobiotic meals, anticipating the ongoing craze for simple, nourishing food".

PEÑA PACHAMAMA

A popular vegan restaurant located in 1630 Powell St, San Francisco, CA 94133, the United States serving Bolivian is accompanied by Latin dance shows, plus a menu of raw vegan fare.

Peña Pachamama is still open after 20 years as a magical, musical world music restaurant in the heart of San Francisco's tourist-happy North Beach neighborhood. The story follows a path of the heart, a successful transformation of a space that used to be San Francisco's most historic speakeasy, and then a beloved Italian eatery called Amelio's. Clark Gable fell in love here with Carole Lombard, some while before Joe DiMaggio enjoyed his wedding dinner with Marilyn Monroe.Now comprising a restaurant, bar, and performance space, the Peña has become what the San Francisco Weekly calls "the friendliest, most inviting nightspot in the city."

Peña Pachamama—One of those magical places... a little island of the future where those who enter her doors are forever transformed by the spirit of the music and dance that takes them in. You'll find it on a little side street in San Francisco's old Latin Quarter somewhere between Chinatown, Fisherman's Wharf, and endless Italian late-night cafes.

It was once one of San Francisco's most important speakeasies; later, Amelio's, which, along with Ernie's, was one of the most famous restaurants in the city. This inviting and comfortable space is where Clark Gable and Carole Lombard had their rendezvous. John & Robert Kennedy, Gary Cooper, Bing Crosby, Dean Martin, and boxer Rocky Marciano were among some of the personalities that frequented this landmark location.

Today, the restaurant serves great food once more, including tasty traditional Bolivian tapas like Plantains and Yucca Frita. We also offer healthy and delicious cooked plant-based or live-food organic samplers.

For something more substantial, try one of our dinner entrees like Gluten-free Lasagna. See our food menu for all of our delicious dining choices.

Reservations are recommended.

Conclusion

I just want to say that you have taken a bold step into becoming a vegan, especially becoming one and maintain it in the famous city of New York. As for how popular the town may be, finding any meal on the street of New York is quite simple and can even be cheap. But finding and eating a vegan meal can be money consuming when compared to eating street junks.

However, looking at the benefits of going vegan, we can't help but overlook its many benefits for both the human body to the environment, animals as well.

Basically, for human health, there are so many benefits of choosing a vegan diet or lifestyle which has been scientifically proven. They include;

- **Rich in specific nutrients;** since vegan foods main consist of and come in the form of whole grains, fruits, vegetables, beans, peas, nuts, and seeds. These foods make up a more significant percentage of a vegan diet than a distinct ordinary diet does so that they can add to an advanced daily intake of some beneficial nutrients. For example, several studies have conveyed that vegan food appears to be better off in potassium, magnesium, folate, and vitamins A, C, and E and also tends to deliver more fiber, antioxidants, and beneficial plant compounds.

- **Weight loss;** many people who are planning to lose weight have resort to doing so by engaging in a vegan diet or become diet. Vegan meals have an average propensity to reduce your human calorie intake of both men and women since most snacks are plant-based. This makes them active in promoting weight loss minus the need to focus on cutting down calorie intake aggressively.

- **Control the risk of cancer;** as stated by the World Health Organization, 'about one-third of all cancers can be barred through what we eat.' vegan food, in general, comprises of more soy products, which may give some shield against breast cancer. Also, eating legumes frequently may diminish the risk of colorectal cancer down to some percentage.

Made in the USA
Las Vegas, NV
09 December 2024

13561113R00056